Antares Stanislas

Tarot Pairings between Major and Minor Arcana

Antares Stanislas Productions

Start of the book:

08/27/2014 at 10.31 hours

©**Copyright**
Tittle of this book: Tarot Pairings between Major and Minor Arcana
Authors: GiampieroTirelli in arte Antares Stanislas
© 2014, GiampieroTirelli
ALL RIGHTS RESERVED. The reproduction, even partial, and by any means, is not allowed without the previous written consent of the author.

Introduction

This title is the second volume of the complete publication "Guide to the Tarot Pairings" composed, too, of a first volume "The Pairings of the Major Arcana". The separation in volumes, as for my books about the meaning of the tarots, is due to the readers' different needs. Some of them use only the major arcana and some others use the full deck. The majority only uses the major arcana. This is the reason why in volume one I wrote about one hundred and twenty pages while in this text I only write about fifty. In volume one, I not only wrote about different pairings, and their interpretation, but I also tried to suggest my own reading technique. In this volume, instead, I ignore that part because who uses the full deck of the tarot, often times, is a person that is already an expert. This person only needs other points of reflection about the reading technique. There will be readers that won't agree with some of my interpretations, this happens to me too when I read other authors, but I remind and warn them, that sometimes a different reading is the result of the subjective meaning that we give to a single tarot. There are, especially in regards of the minor arcana, many divergences of opinions about their meanings. In the major arcana the non-uniformity of the meaning is less evident. I maintain that the purchaser of this title will know the value of the tarots being propaedeutic in every study of the pairings. Like I wrote, in particular cases, the reader may find it hard to understand my readings, but it is only because he/she gives a subjective value to the tarot that is different from mine. In this specific case, I will refer them to my text "Minor Arcana Tarot, their meaning without learning it by heart" where I explain my thoughts, and subjective meaning, of each minor arcana. In this volume, I omit the pictures of the arcana, too, leaving more room for the text. In specific, the images are not very helpful. My point of view is that each tarot, of any deck, should have the same meaning. Each author that writes about tarot changes symbols and images in a single card but this does not change the real meaning for the scope of the reading. As I wrote in volume one, it is impossible to write a book that includes all the possible pairings, which are 462, considering those composed only of two cards, (ignoring the orientation, otherwise they would be many more), and 9240 considering the pairings formed by three cards. The reader should not think that the proposed examples are few. In this volume two, for every major arcane, in fact, I will write around eight parings and I will write around ten pairings for every minor arcane; in the final result the minor arcane will be involved almost 200 times (22 minor arcana X 9, the average number of examples), observing like this, in practice, all or almost all 56 minor arcana. In this way there will be the chance to observe how all the minor arcana react when they are close to a major arcane, in either case, when one of the cards is extracted from the right or reversed. I give a practical example. If in this text we use the minor arcane of three of swords for a total number of four readings/examples, the reader will be able to perceive by intuition how to interpret such a minor arcane even when it is extracted from close by to other major arcana, not involved in the previous examples. As I wrote in previous lines, this volume 2, together with volume 1, form my book "Complete Guide to the Tarot Pairings" for a total of almost 180 pages, a very respectable book.

The Fool

-Fool followed by the five of cups reversed: a love story without stability. A confusing situation, that wears down our sensitivity. Contradictions.

-Fool followed by the two of cups with the three of swords: a restricted or unstable love that is passing through a moment of physical and/or moral separation. A moment of moral crisis that requires our physical or spiritual distancing.

-Five of swords followed by the fool reversed and by the six of cups: it is the end of an emotional situation. We are living a sad moment and in the memories of the past. Looking for a balanced moral state after a loss or defeat.

-queen of swords followed by the fool and by the King of swords: A confusing situation with a partner. In the positive sense, the spread itself indicates that the couple is planning a new beginning about which they are still not certain. At work, it can indicate a shallow relationship with a coworker or a complicated one with an employer.

-ace of batons followed by the fool and by the seven of coins: a new job or the execution of an action that will give results that won't satisfy us or lead to contrasts.

-fool followed by the ten of coins and by the ace of coins: despite of our immaturity, inherent to the question asked by the consultant, the reading is "positive", everything will go for the best, especially if the question is inherent to money, work or material matters. While for the feelings the reading will be equally positive even though the true feelings leave room for the concreteness/materiality/chance.

-Knight of cups followed by the fool reversed and the nine of swords: an agony or emotional issue that causes anxiety.

The Magician

-ace of batons followed by the magician reversed: We are getting ready to find a job, we are moving to reach a goal, but it is not the moment, our efforts are being blocked or delayed.

-magician followed by the two of cups: we meet a new person, we live a new start. Very good if the question is related to love or emotions.

-ace of coins followed by the magician and by the five of coins: we want to do something new but what will it cost us? In moral or material terms?

-the magician followed by the ace of swords: in the positive case, the cards invite to be firm towards a new beginning, but frequently the pairing indicates the start of a challenge and in the case that the ace is reversed we could be seeing a real conflict.

-magician reversed followed by the eight of swords and by the three of swords: possibly a fraud, a false communication. We are victims of the circumstances and when we are not it would be better to postpone our actions.

-magician with the two or three of batons: excellent initiatives that provide for possible associations and concreteness

-magician followed by the three and by the four of cups: a flirting situation can become something concrete. A betrothal can change in cohabitation. A hope that concretizes and brings us moral relief.

-magician followed by the eight of coins reversed: we want to start a new path or activity, but then will we be ready to provide support for our creation?

The Papess

-papess reversed followed by the three of swords reversed: removal, separation, retirement, are the words that are more suitable for this pairing.

-papess reversed followed by the three of coins: anxiety because of a communication that we are waiting for or because of moral or material matters.

-papess followed by the two of cups and by the five of swords: the aspirations of the couple to be happy but with a great fear of defeat.

-papess followed by the nine of swords and by the ace of batons reversed: fears that block every action.

-papess reversed followed by the ten of swords: spiritual suffering and it could be physical too.

-papess followed by the queen of swords reversed: their positions are maintained in a decisive, stubborn and conservative manner.

-papess followed by the five of coins reversed: a morally betrayed person. A person (even a male one if the question is made by a man and does not involve entities from the opposite sex) that is spiritually poor.

-three of cups followed by the papess and by the four of cups: the urge to build something, of putting into practice their own thoughts and mood.

-papess followed by the seven of coins and by the three of cups reversed: it can indicate a moral or material conflict of interest. The conflict can be internal, like this arcane seems to indicate.

The Empress

-seven of coins reversed followed by the empress: with determination and pragmatism they will manage to defeat their enemy or reach an agreement.

-empress followed by the two of swords: a woman with doubts, a concrete situation or that wants to be put in place not without incertitudes.

-empress followed by the four of swords: a danger for waiting or delaying before executing their projects or thoughts. Problems with a woman in the domestic or workplace environments

-empress with the three of coins: the start of a new Project that has yet to materialize, the desire of giving life to a new idea.

-three of swords followed by the empress and the eight of cups reversed: we have been wronged or we are disappointed by the matter. Despite our desire of doing and moving forward, we do everything with apathy.

-empress reversed followed by the seven of cups: a new acquaintance to distrust, especially if who asks the question is a man. A woman that has seen her wishes betrayed. Even in the case that the empress was extracted in the correct orientation and the seven of cups was reversed, the substance of the reading would not have changed.

-empress followed by the two of batons reversed: a woman that feels remorse and/or regrets with respect to the question asked. In general, the pairing indicates actions and thoughts opposed by people or circumstances.

-six of swords followed by the empress: an unstable period in our lives where, despite the research for equilibrium, we will carry our ideas and actions.

The Emperor

-emperor followed by the five of swords and by the empress. A conflict or detachment in the couple. In the specific case that the cards were extracted in the right orientation this gives hope. In the case that one or more of the cards were extracted reversed, the reading would have been more "negative".

-emperor followed by the knave of cups: collaboration between father and son or with a person with whom we have emotional links. An infatuated man. Pleasant news or communications.

-emperor followed by the seven of cups reversed: a man to distrust if the question is asked by a woman, otherwise a deluded man. An idea of false concreteness, which we should not trust, for now.

-six of coins reversed followed by the emperor reversed and by the three of cups reversed: a precarious situation, to which the emperor seems not be able to stand firmly and solidly.

-emperor followed by the three of cups reversed: A solidity or sought-after stability is probably obtained at the expense of morality or a true affection.

-emperor followed by the knight of batons: unpleasant news are coming. We are made aware of a displeasing situation. Now we are sure.

-emperor followed by the knight of coins: indicates a concrete action or news that confirm our hopes. It is more valid for material matters than for affective ones.

-emperor followed by the four of coins: a situation that is steadily becoming true.

The Pope

-pope followed by the four of coins: conservative spirit, desire for concreteness and stability. A vocation or ideal that is linked to material things.

-pope followed by the knight of swords: a strong-willed person, a decision made after a long reflection.

-pope followed by the three of swords reversed: a spiritual detachment from the situation. Not being lived with suffering by with full awareness. A suitor from far away that we should not trust or causes irritation.

-pope followed by the two of coins: arrival of news, desire to change the essence of the current situation. The thought of several choices with tendency towards being conservative.

-pope reversed followed by the ace of batons reversed: there are not hopes towards changing, the person seems to have a blocked spirit despite their initiatives.

-pope reversed followed by the seven of coins: associations that does not gratify us. A person that is an obstacle. We are disappointed because of useless efforts.

-pope reversed followed by the six of coins reversed: person disappointed by the everyday life, by their state of being, obviously in the requested domain.

-pope followed by the ace of cups: morale at good levels, a flirt, a person in love.

-pope followed by the four of cups: a feel or stable situation that provides calmness, sincere person, trustable.

The Lovers

-lovers followed by the three of cups: emotional situation that provides hope or happiness. Decision made with the heart and that brings joy.

-lovers followed by the two of cups and by the three of cups: relationship or concrete association. Good news.

-lovers followed by the queen of coins: relationship or infatuation towards a concrete person or that works in commerce. Reversed, decision dictated by concrete scopes, rational, materialistic person.

-lovers followed by the ace of batons: sexual attraction. The action that brings a decision.

-lovers reversed followed by the five of coins reversed: poverty of feelings, treason, extra money. A direction chosen or undertaken causes some problems.

-lovers followed by the eight of coins: a project wants to concretize, emotional or material, according to the requested domain.

-lovers followed by the King of swords reversed: emotional situation with a detached or cold person. Decision made with too much stubbornness.

-lovers followed by the seven of swords reversed: a couple's or at work reconciliation after frictions or due to some other person.

-lovers followed by the two of swords: a love, a flirt, a decisión, not without doubts and fears.

The Chariot

-chariot followed by the three of batons: the concretization of an action or thought. Sometimes it also expresses the creation of thoughts, their fertilization.

-chariot followed by the ten of swords reversed: a trip that gives us physical and/or moral troubles, accompanied by opposition.

-chariot followed by the knight of cups: a move for emotional or affective reasons. A creative thinking that procures us happiness or our serenity.

-chariot reversed followed by the three of swords reversed: a postponed travel or move. Physical or moral detachment.

- four of swords followed by the chariot reversed: the end of a sojourn. Problems in the family, postponed actions.

-chariot followed by the seven of swords reversed: victory against adversaries or calumnies. A contract with good ending.

-nine of coins followed by the chariot: material serenity, new and joyful changes or actions that are work related.

-nine of swords reversed followed by the chariot: despite our fears, doubts and anxiety, we bring our will to completeness

-chariot followed by the five of batons or by the four of cups: we have won a dispute. Despite opposition and disputes we manage to carry our attempt.

The Justice

-justice followed by the two of cups reversed: A couple's light crisis. A relationship or lawful association with little moral satisfaction.

-justice followed by the two of cups: a new encounter. a bureaucratic matter that turns in our favor. Ps: it is a pairing that suggests great feelings.

-justice followed by the ace of swords: the start of a case or controversy. The ace of swords reversed emphasizes the reading.

-justice followed by the five of swords on the right orientation or reversed: a Pyrrhic victory. Lack of equilibrium with respect to the matter.

-justice followed by the knave of swords: bureaucratic news or their execution. Person that looks for equilibrium.

- two of coins followed by justice reversed: a change or decision or communication that makes us anxious.

-justfice followed by the four of coins: a judgement in our favor. The found-again equilibrium.

-justice followed by the eight of cups reversed: we are not happy, desire of change the current status of being followed by the anxiety or indecision of doing it.

-justice followed by the knight of coins and by the eight swords: decisions to which we have to answer with sacrifices and responsibility.

The Hermit

-Hermit followed by the three of cups: a love that consolidates with time.

-hermit reversed followed by the three of cups: emotional crisis, moral or physical detachment.

-hermit followed by the three of cups reversed: emotional crisis that could finish after a short period of detachment. Relationship undertaken against their true feelings.

-hermit followed by the five of coins: moment of loneliness or crisis, emotional or material, according to the question of the requestor.

-hermit reversed followed by the five of coins reversed: economical or emotional crisis, debts and loses.

-hermit followed by the King of coins: a stalled decision, dictated by rationality or material issues. A wise person.

-hermit reversed followed by the queen of swords: a hostile person. The end of a love story because of cheating. An irrevocable physical and/or moral detachment for the entire duration of the spread.

-six of coins reversed followed by the hermit: it takes time and all our wisdom to comply in time with our daily problems and regain a balance inherent to the sector requested.

-hermit followed by the ace of batons reversed: voluntary retirement. Temporary stall, positive, of our own goals.

-hermit reversed followed by the three of swords reversed: end of a relationship, physical or moral detachment.

The Wheel of Fortune

-wheel followed by the queen of coins: turning point in the work sector. In the emotional field there will be a new encounter or evolution in the relationship.

-wheel followed by the three of cups reversed: positive development, partnership, at the expense of their own moral or material gratification.

-wheel followed by the knave of batons: concrete development of a thought. Good news.

-wheel of fortune followed by the seven of cups reversed: A positive development that hides a possible delusion, be careful.

-wheel followed by the three or four of cups: development of a relationship or a new encounter that brings joy and/or stability.

-wheel followed by the ace of coins: incoming money, a new flirt where the word 'love' is still virtual. A pairing that promises good things.

-wheel followed by the two of swords: positive development (that looks like that) of the matter which, however, still leaves us with doubts or anxiety.

-wheel followed by the ten of batons: positive development in the sector requested that required the assuming of commitments and responsibilities.

-wheel followed by the eight of coins: a new project, a new job. The concretization of the same one.

The Strength

-strength followed by the five of cups: desire to continue with a path despite disappointments or regrets.

-strength followed by the five of coins and the six of coins: desire to overcome the adversity with spirit and abnegation.

-strength followed by the eight of cups and by the two of swords: desire to continue; persevere, despite many doubts and a state of being that does not gratify us.

-strength followed by the knight of swords: desire of adventure. Will to carry a decisive action, impulsive. A person that loves adventure.

-strength followed by the eight of batons and by the ten of batons: commitments (even if expensive or strenuous) are carried out or completed.

-strength reversed followed by the five of swords reversed: wasted effort, tenacity without reason to exist. Banging their heads against the wall leads nowhere.

-strength followed by the two of batons and by the ace of batons. Will to act, to join, new initiatives.

-strength followed by the three of swords reversed and four of swords: will to detach from the situation or take distance. Physical or moral separation, often wanted.

-strength followed by the ten of coins: successful actions, the thoughts become concrete. Will to emerge.

The Hanged Man

-the hanged man followed by the three of cups: costly material or moral commitment in terms of achieving the project or idea.

-three of swords followed by the hanged man: a moral or physical detachment that brings sadness.

-the hanged man followed by the eight of swords: we have little chance of changing the events, it will be normal, instead, suffer them assuming a state of impotence.

-the hanged man reversed followed by the knave of swords: no positive news, a person that puts us in a bad mood.

-the hanged man followed by the six of cups reversed: emotional blockage that affects the present due to memories or experiences of the past.

-the hanged man followed by the queen of cups: a love that requires some sacrifice. A dreamer woman, timid.

-the hanged man followed by the knight of cups: temporary emotional or material issues, we move to resolve them. An altruistic person, of sacrifice.

-five of coins followed by the hanged man reversed: debts or existential crisis. Sacrifices to be made.

-four of cups followed by the hanged man: need to adapt to the situation to achieve stability or concreteness.

The Death

-death followed by the ace of coins and by the two of coins: a choice, a contract, news that bring our desire for change.

-death followed by the six of coins: we want a change from our current situation that won't gratify us a lot.

- five of swords followed by the death reversed: emotional detachment, a negative pairing for the requested sector.

-death followed by the ten of swords: strive to improve their physical and mental state. If one of the two cards is reversed, the pairing emphasizes what is written.

-death followed by the ace of swords: situation that evolves, start of a discussion or conflict. If one of the cards is extracted reversed it is probably a negative change in the situation.

-Ace of swords followed by the death: the conclusion of a dispute or an action or thought.

-death followed by the queen of swords: a widow, a person that is single, an emotional change. If one of the cards is extracted reversed, it can indicate an enemy or damages by an enemy person.

-death followed by the ten of coins reversed: sorrows in the family, an aborted or incomplete project.

-death followed by the ace of batons reversed: wasted efforts.

The Temperance

-temperance reversed followed by the knave of swords reversed: a person that puts us in a bad mood. Balance to be found. Unpleasant news, documents, communications, scarce, blocked, or delayed.

-temperance followed by the King of batons or by the queen of batons: a slow action, a methodical person, balanced. Elaborated decisions that need time, but very balanced. A communicative, balanced, calmed, sociable, esteemed, progressive person.

-temperance followed by the five of coins reversed: find oneself after a "poo" period.

-temperance followed by the nine of swords: with time we'll find again the lost balance.

-temperance followed by the eight of coins: a slow project, that requires time, concreteness in their own job or ideas.

-seven of coins followed by the temperance: dissatisfactions, we do not feel fully gratified by our expectations.

-temperance followed by the five of cups reversed: apathy due to emotional or moral matters derived from practical situations.

-temperance followed by the eight of batons: an actions that requires decision, speed, that cannot wait.

-temperance with the eight of batons reversed: an impulsive action that requires processing, time.

The Devil

-devil followed by the two of cups: a passion, or association of interest.

-devil followed by the seven of swords reversed: devious enemies. Do not trust colleagues, associates, or problems with them.

-devil followed by a card with a character like a knave, knight, king or queen: a strategic person, materialistic, not very altruistic.

-devil reversed followed by a card with a character (as mentioned above): deceptions suffered, fraud, moral or material damage, enemies, unreliable persons or enemy.

-devil followed by the three of coins and by the ten of cups: strategy that leads to success and high morale.

-devil reversed followed by an ace of cups: relationship towards material purposes and opportunism that is not for sincere affection.

-devil followed by four of coins: greed, love for money or their social position.

-devil reversed followed by the nine of swords and by the eight of swords: mental blockage, anxiety, and torments. Deceptions or situations that have left their mark.

-devil followed by the nine of batons: annoyances that come from the adversity of more or less "transparent-clear issues"

The Tower

-tower followed by the eight of swords: a change that is stalled or delayed. Impediment to move or act.

-tower followed by the three of batons: change in the negotiations or terms of a contest or project. If the three of batons is reversed, it can be added to the interruption of the negotiations, the dialog.

-tower followed by the five of swords: the defeat or change that brings disappointment.

-three of swords reversed followed by the tower: moral or material distancing. Separation.

-tower followed by the two of swords: discussions or problems because of doubts, decisions, and uncertainties, differences of ideas.

-queen of swords followed by the tower: a person that can cause us problems. A firm change with great power of will.

-tower followed by the ten of batons reversed: problems in carrying out their commitments.

-tower followed by the three of coins reversed: blocked communications, blurred contracts. A delayed project.

-tower followed by the knight of batons: transfer, arrival of bad news, impulsive person, adventures.

-tower followed by the knave of coins reversed: no concrete ideas, news that are delayed or don't arrive, a person with many projects or promises that are not very concrete or that cannot keep.

The Star

-star followed by the ace of cups and by the two of cups: Birth of a flirt or a happy event that raises our morale

-star followed by the ten of batons reversed: the hope and the illusion of resolving the commitments that are beginning to weigh too much, physically or materially.

-star followed by the seven of coins: the hope of signing a contract, of creating an association, of a better financial stage.

-star followed by the queen of cups: a flirt, an emotional bond, a thought of love.

-star followed by the five of swords reversed: utopias, bad choices that have an impact on the moral state.

-star followed by the knave of coins: positive news that were expected and in which there was hope. New ideas for new businesses.

-four of batons followed by the star reversed and by the two of cups: a relationship that loses its own stability, situation to be reviewed (for the requested sector)

-star followed by the King of cups reversed: A person who deceives, false illusions. A choice to rationalize.

-star followed by the nine of coins: they reap the rewards of a project, "heavy" situations that become lighter.

The Moon

-moon followed by the two of swords: too many doubts assail the consultant. Lack transparency in some issues.

-the two of swords followed by the moon reversed: a deception suffered, gossips, a hostile person.

-moon followed by the king of batons: a person on which we should no trust, not completely transparent. Confusing actions

-nine of swords reversed followed by the moon reversed: depressive state, very anxious, the person amplifies its problems or senses them severely.

-three of coins followed by the six of coins and by the moon: the situation improves, but not everything is perfect, there remain doubts to dissipate as soon as possible.

-any character arcane like a knave, knight, King and queen extracted reversed together with the moon: A person in which to distrust.

-moon followed by the three of swords: the fears, the difficult situation, separate or block the person or the matter.

-moon followed by the three of cups reversed: possible love triangle, or suspicion of the same. Avoid lust of excesses to prevent disappointments. Anonymous communications.

-moon reversed followed by the two of batons: regret, remorse, they feel a moral state that is not easy.

-moon followed by the eight of swords reversed and ace of batons reversed: stall or blockage of the matter.

The Sun

-three of cups followed by the ace of cups and by the sun: start of a relationship or collaboration. A moral state that is getting better.

-sun followed by the ten of batons and by the three of coins: an issue that is being carried out despite the fatigue for the commitments. Reports, contracts, collaborations, projects, that are brought forward.

-sun followed by the nine of cups: optimism, thoughts of love, ambitious thoughts turned to his own personal growth.

-sun followed by any knight: an action brought to fruition or that will be undertaken, positive news, a pleasure trip or physical distancing.

-sun followed by any character like the King or queen: sunny person, of energy, charisma, that helps us, decisive.

- sun followed by any knave: the beginning of a constructive thought, of a challenge. A cheerful person, radiant. News that we waited, happy communications or to be undertaken.

-any King of queen reversed followed by the sun: victory over enemies, a person who hinders us. Our own moral or physical recovery.

-sun followed by the ten of coins: the realization of a project. Peace in the family, especially in the subject matter if the question is specific about money.

-sun followed by the two of swords: recovery despite the fact that some doubts / contrast remains.

The Judgement

-judgement followed by the six of cups: The possible return of a love, resume of a relationship, an old question.

-judgement reversed followed by the three of swords: change in the situation with possible worsening. Communications interrupted or cold.

-judgement followed by the seven of coins: recovery, the situation gets better even though it does not gratify us completely.

-judgement followed by the eight and by the nine of coins: the realization of a project, the signing of a contract, and his material or moral well-being. In matters of love it indicates a more concrete project but not the index of affection between partners.

-ace of swords reversed followed by the judgement: an old argument emerges, legal communications, bureaucratic, conflicting.

-judgement reversed followed by the four of swords reversed: It indicates the end of all things, of course inherent to the question asked. Wait for better times.

-judgement followed by the eight of cups and by the seven of cups: Change in love due to discontent, little gratification. But be careful, though, to not get too excited, for the moment.

-two of coins followed by the judgement and by the four of cups: a contract, a communication, a change that brings us optimism or personal gratification.

-judgement followed by the four of batons: looking for a change that will lead to something concrete.

The World

-world followed by the two of batons: contracts that are brought to fruition, the action directed to the association.

-world followed by the five of coins: recovery from a difficult period with respect to the requested sector.

-world followed by the five of swords reversed: incomplete situations, not gratifying.

-world followed by any character of king or queen: realization of a project. Meeting with a person who helps or completes us. Ourselves in a position of advantage.

-world followed by any character of horse: news that outline the issue, action taken that leads to conclusion. A friend. A shift.

-world followed by any knave reversed: Despite delays or incidents or negative news we have, now, a complete view of the situation.

-five of batons followed by the world: diatribes that end, the end of the opposition or the victory over themselves and the people who created them.

-world followed by the seven of batons: the end of the contracts, the struggles. Courage and overcoming of obstacles.

-world followed by the eight or by the nine of batons: victory or position of recovery (fast enough) from the obstacles.

-world followed by the six of batons: victory over the deceptions, insults, uncertainties, everyday problems.

Index

Introduction   pag.3

The Fool   pag.7

The Magician   pag.9

The Papess   pag.11

The Empress   pag.13

The Emperor   pag.15

The Pope   pag.17

The Lovers	pag.19
The Chariot	pag.21
The Justice	pag.23
The Hermit	pag.25
The Wheel of fortune	pag.27
The Strength	pag.29
The Man Hanged	pag.31
The Death	pag.33

The Temperance	pag.35
The Devil	pag.37
The Tower	pag.39
The Star	pag.41
The Moon	pag.43
The Sun	pag.45
The Judgement	pag.47
The World	pag.49

Bibliography Antares Stanislas

- Practical Cartomancy for All (ita)
- Major Arcana Tarot. Their meaning without learning it by heart. Vol 1 (ita)
- Minor Arcana Tarot. Their meaning without learning it by heart. Vol 2 (ita)
- Tarot the prediction of the future. Major and Minor Arcana Vol 1 + Vol 2 (ita)
- Predictive astrology. Events under x-rays. (ita)
- Predictive astrology. The new discovery. Reading method of a transit (ita & esp)
- Pairing of Major Arcana tarot. Vol 1 (ita & esp)
- Pairing of Major and Minor Arcana. Vol 2 (ita & esp)
- Tarot pairings, a complete guide. Vol 1 + Vol 2 (ita &esp)